Pubwalks in the Cotswolds

Whether you are new to walking or looking for a challenge you will have no difficulty in following these footpaths and bridle ways to a worthwhile watering hole."

Easy to follow and never too far, each walk is laid out in such a way that planning your "pub stop" is simplicity itself.

This book will take you to traditional pubs and inns where you can be sure of a friendly "Cotswold" welcome.

Colin Handy

Published by
REARDON PUBLISHING
PO BOX 919
CHELTENHAM, GL50 9AN
Tel: 01242 231800
Website: www.reardon.co.uk
Email: reardon@bigfoot.com

Copyright © 2003
REARDON PUBLISHING
2nd Edition 2006

Written and researched by Colin Handy
Walks taken from the Gloucestershire Citizen's popular
"Shanks's Pony" series of Pub Walks.

Text Copyright © 2003
Colin Handy

ISBN 1 873877 62 5
9781873877623

Edited by Hilary Allison

Maps by Colin Handy

Test Walked and updated by Bob Cox

Cover Design by Nicholas Reardon

Photographs by Colin Handy, Julia Craig
and Nicholas Reardon

Cartoons and Illustrations by Peter T. Reardon

Layout and Design by Nicholas Reardon

Printed by
STOATE & BISHOP (PRINTERS) LTD,
Cheltenham, Gloucestershire.

INDEX

Walk 1 - Asthall to Widford

Distance: 3[1/2] miles Allow: 1[1/2] hours

"A stroll through open farmland, beginning and ending in one of Oxfordshire's quaintest villages. With a varied landscape and two pubs for a rest, this is a very different walk, best kept for a summer's day."

Asthall lies about three miles west of Burford and has been described as "a classic Windrush village, complete with water meadows, willow trees, a gabled Elizabethan manor overlooking a small church and a tidy little inn". That "tidy little inn" is the "Maytime Inn" which is your starting point for this memorable walk.

Whether you choose to visit the pub now or on your return, you will not be disappointed as it offers a wide selection of "real ales" and boasts an extensive menu. Don't forget however that there is a second pub on this short walk which could affect your timing!

"Maytime Inn"

Leave the pub on your left and walk up to the triangle where you turn left, passing Downham Cottage on your left. As you leave Asthall you pass a row of lime trees on your right and soon take the left hand fork at the 'Y' junction, heading for an old stone bridge over the River Windrush.

Cross the river bridge and immediately go over a stone stile on your left where a finger post points you in the direction of the village of Swinbrook. As you follow the well trodden path across the lush meadows, take your time to savour the picture postcard view to the left, back over Asthall and its limestone buildings.

Already it's an easy and pleasant walk alongside the Windrush whose waters have carved a crazy path through the fields. Your path takes you at a right angle across the field and is well marked with yellow arrows, leading you towards a set of small cottages in the distance.

This is a very popular walk and you will rarely be alone in your journey. As you head for two more stiles in the far right hand corner of the field. On the horizon, to your left you can see the traffic frantically passing along the busy A40 Cheltenham to Oxford road which seems like another world away.

Keeping the dry stone wall on your right, cross the stiles and continue on the path which now takes you slightly left to your next point of call, the second pub on the walk, the "Swan Inn" at Swinbook.

Yet again this is a pub straight out of yesteryear complete with flag stone floors and a stable door. The dark interior is a haven on a hot day and warmly welcoming in the winter. With its drinks and food selection to rival the "Maytime Inn", you are spoilt for choice on today's walk.

Leaving the pub on your left, walk carefully up the narrow road, ignoring the road to your right, into the delightful village of Swinbrook, a neatly proportioned place with a most unusual church.

This is the traditional home of the famous Mitford family whose daughters Nancy and Unity are buried in the chuchyard. Within this curious church a surprise awaits in the form of a pair of "three-decker" wall tombs dedicated to the memory of another local family, the Fettiplaces.

Leave the church on your left and continue carefully up the road taking you out of Swinbrook. Note the pretty little ford on your right fed from the fast flowing brook that now keeps you company as you climb with the road. After a quarter of a mile you turn left at the 'Y' junction to pass Walnut Tree House on your right.

Now take your time as the narrow road becomes quite steep before eventually flattening out once more. At the top of the climb someone has thoughtfully provided a bench which makes an ideal stopping place for a snack and to catch your breath and take in the panoramic view over this corner of Oxfordshire.

The walk along the road becomes very easy and offers fine views to your left and right. The dry stone wall on your left eventually grows to a magnificent six feet in height and when it ends, look for a well marked footpath on your left. A stile takes you off the road and into a lush valley as you now descend towards Widford through a scene that for all the world could be Scotland.

At the bottom of the valley go over a stile and after 100 yards you turn left on a well used footpath taking you back into Swinbrook. However before you take this path look to your right where in the ajoining field stands the tiny church of

St.Oswald which dates back to the 13th century and boasts some fine examples of medieval wall paintings. Thanks to its monastic connections with Gloucester the parcel of land around this church was until fairly recently classed as "Gloucestershire" despite the fact it is well into Oxfordshire.

As you re-join the path to Swinbrook, take your time to reflect upon some of the surrounding sights. Locals will tell you that the trees around here are known as the "hanging trees" as men and women convicted at Gloucester Assizes were brought here on their final journey, to be hanged.

The area is also believed to have been home to a band of highway robbers who lived just below the church. These men were also said to be gamblers and, as you pass alongside the church along a lane of small cobbles, look carefully at the intricate designs depicting the four card suits of Hearts, Diamonds, Clubs and Spades. It is a pity and a sad reflection of our modern life to see the damage inflicted on the Clubs' symbol by one of the local utility services.

Now it is time to retrace your steps on this short walk, back to the ancient "Swan Inn" and on to Asthall and another chance to rest at the "Maytime Inn".

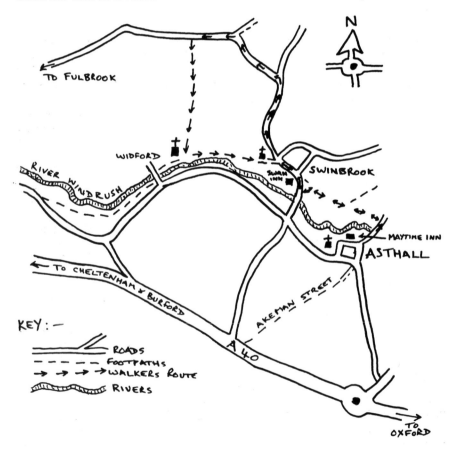

KEY : —
— ROADS
— — — — FOOTPATHS
→ → → →WALKERS ROUTE
∼∼∼∼ RIVERS

Walk 2 - Birdlip to Brimpsfield

Distance: 4 miles Allow: 2 hours

"A country ramble through open farmland, beginning and ending in a once busy village. This walk offers a varied landscape and a stylish pub for a rest. An easy walk which is mainly flat but has a deceptively testing end."

Park the car in Birdlip village close to the local primary school and out of the way of local residential parking.

Birdlip suffered for decades at the endless mercy of the motor car but now wallows in the peaceful splendour that its by-pass has brought. It is a village well worth wandering around either before or after the walk and its local pub the "Royal George Hotel" remains a popular stopping off place for a drink or a meal.

Begin the walk in the centre of the village and take the minor country road marked "Brimpsfield". You will stay on the road for some distance and need to take care as it carries quite a lot of local traffic.

Within a few short minutes you are into the Cotswold countryside and high on a ridge. To emphasise the fact, there is a "Trig" point just a few yards off to your right marking the highest point on the hilly escarpment. There is a Gloucestershire feel to the whole landscape with rich farmland dotted with honey coloured houses and barns.

After about a quarter of a mile turn right on a minor road for Caudle Green and follow the road as it sweeps left and gentle rises. Off to your left are fine valley views and above this the old Roman Road "Ermin Street", now called the A417(T), with its constant hum of traffic.

Pass Blacklaines Farm on your left and after a further 50 yards leave the road and turn left on a well marked and well used bridle way. Go through two gates and continue straight ahead with the hedge on your right. The walking remains flat and very easy.

When the hedge ends, follow the fence to a metal gate. Here you re-join the road and turn right. The road rises gently uphill to sweep left into the village.

Follow the road into the heart of Brimpsfield until you have the War Memorial on your right. Here you leave the road and cross the road following the well marked path to the church.

As you walk along the concrete path towards the Church of St. Michael you begin to see the earth walls and old moat that once protected a castle on this site. Unfortunately the land is private and you can only guess at the history of the castle. It was mentioned in "The Doomsday Book". Its last owner was John Giffard who took a stand against Edward II's misrule in 1322 and was hanged at Gloucester for his troubles with an order that the castle be raised to the ground.

The church however is well worth a visit and is reached through an avenue of trees and a series of arches formed from them. It is essentially Norman and most unusual in its design, its churchyard offering a splendid view of the valley below.

Retrace your steps to the church gate and turn right to cross the field to find a stile in the dry stone wall. Cross the stile and follow the path down the field to the bottom left hand corner where you again go over a stile to join a minor road, turn right and follow the road downhill.

As the road starts to sweep around to the right, leave it and go over a stile on your left, following the yellow arrow marker. This track will lead you to your resting place at the pub. Take note of the spot as you will have to re-trace your steps to the stile after your leisurely stop.

Drop down the field and after 20 yards cross a stile on your right before turning sharp left and making your way steeply downhill. At certain times of the year this section can get quite muddy and you may need to come prepared.

At the bottom of the slope, keep the dry stone wall and hedge on your left and walk straight ahead, up the rise of the field. Just before the top of the slope go through an old farm gate and then continue straight ahead keeping the trees on your left.

"Golden Heart"

Skirt around the final trees and you should now be able to see the garden of the "Golden Heart" public house just ahead of you. This is Nettleton Bottom and your stopping off point. The "Golden Heart" is an ancient pub and you will not be disappointed with what you find. The pub has been tastefully refurbished over the years and offers a fine restaurant and bar offering a wide variety of "real ale" beers and an extensive menu.

From the pub retrace your steps to the minor road, cross the stile onto the road and turn right, heading for the village. Now make your way up the hill, taking your time as the climb is steep after the pleasant stop. Very soon you pass the church on your left.

At the top of the slope, with the Brimpsfield village sign just ahead of you, leave the road and turn right to make your way down a little track to a metal farm gate. Go through the gate and after 10 yards turn left towards a little copse on your right.

Now you need to exercise great care as the way is poorly marked.

Follow the stony track downhill, keeping the trees on your right and loop around the copse heading for the farm gate at the bottom of the slope. When you get to the gate you will find another gate on your left. Go through this left-hand gate and make your way steadily across the centre of the field at a slight right angle. The stile that you are looking for is about 200 yards ahead in the hedgerow on your right.

Go over the stile and turn left, following the yellow arrow signs, keeping the hedge on your left. Again you need to exercise great care to follow the route. Do not leave this field but follow the hedge at a slight right angle. At this point you should have a modern house on your left and a derelict building off to your right.

Slightly off to your right is a small wood and the line of the path takes you up to the far corner of the wood. The stile that you are now looking for is just beyond the wood, on your right hand side.

Go over the stile on your right and walk straight ahead, keeping to the left side of the field. Pass the waterworks on your left and continue straight ahead until you come to an old water tank and a wide track. Turn right onto the track and walk the short distance to the houses ahead of you.

The track passes between the houses to a metal farm gate which you go through. After 10 yards you join a metalled road and turn left. This minor road now takes you back into the centre of Birdlip village, offering you a second chance to visit the "Royal George Hotel".

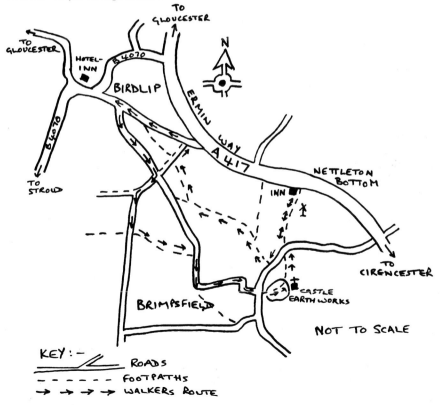

Walk 3 Bulls Cross to Slad

Distance: 3[1/2] miles Allow: 2 hours

"A pleasantly different walk taking in well stocked woodland, open valleys and rolling hills with unrestricted views. A chance to linger in an old, traditional pub and wallow in the Gloucestershire countryside which is known worldwide as the land of 'Cider With Rosie'."

The walk starts at Bulls Cross on the B4070 Stroud to Birdlip road where you can safely park the car off the road. Cross the road with care turn left and begin to make your way towards the Stroud. Cross the junction with the Painswick road and after a further 15 yards leave the road and follow a well marked bridle way off to your right. You are walking on a wide dirt track parallel with the road and heading towards a well stocked wood, this is Frith Wood, a nature reserve cared for by The Gloucestershire Trust.

The bridle way takes you through an avenue of trees with a fine view on your right of Painswick and its surrounding villages nestling in the lush valley below. In the winter months the path can get muddy so appropriate footwear will be needed.

Frith Wood is a fine example of an ancient Cotswold beech wood, designated as a site of special scientific interest. Beech and Ash trees dominate the area with a sprinkling of Oak, Yew, Whitebeam, Field Maple and Elm. Some flowers that you may see are Lesser Periwinkle and Bird's-Orchid, depending upon the time of year.

Do not deviate from the broad track as there are minor paths going off in all directions. The walking now becomes flat and easy as you walk away from the busy road and the wood is suddenly quiet and peaceful.

At the top of the long slope the path narrows and begins to follow the edge of the wood with fields and a dry-stone wall on your right. You eventually leave the wood through an old wooden gate and enter a field to continue straight ahead, still with the wall on your right.

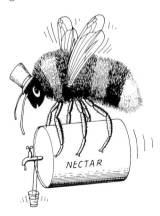

Here the views suddenly open up to your left offering a marvellous sight down over Slad and the deep green valleys protecting it, with their rolling hills dotted with livestock. This is a place to just linger for a while and let the world go by.

At the end of the field continue straight ahead on the wide stone track, heading towards a large barn. Again the walking is easy as you follow the flat track, between the fields along the ridge.

As you pass Worgans Farm Cottages on your right the track becomes metalled. Continue for a further 20 yards and leave the track by crossing a wooden stile on your left onto a well signed path.

You now begin to drop downhill, keeping a stone wall on your left and a fence on your right. Off to the right distant views of Stroud begin to open up as you follow the path which snakes down through the trees. Go through a rather complicated wooden stile and continue to follow the path as it steeply descends the field to eventually leave it in the bottom left hand corner, through a metal gate.

You are now in "Cider With Rosie" country, the home of author Laurie Lee, and it is easy to imagine him having his famous childhood adventures in these very fields.

Continue to drop steeply downhill on a wide, stony track for a further 50 yards when you leave the track on your right and follow a narrow footpath, marked with a yellow arrow, down to the road. Cross the road with great care and turn left to follow the pavement into the village of Slad.

Here is your opportunity to take a break at the famous old "free house", the "Woolpack", a pub straight out of yesteryear. Its two small bars offer "real ales" and snacks and a unique opportunity to rub shoulders with true country folk. If the weather is nice there is a small terraced garden from where you can enjoy the sight of the green valley fields.

From the pub continue through the village on the footpath alongside the B4070 heading towards Cheltenham. Slad has a true mixture of architectural styles, ranging from old Cotswold stone cottages to modern houses with all of their comforts.

When the footpath ends turn right into Steanbridge Lane and start to drop down the hill on the minor road as it winds its way between the houses. At the 'Y' junction stay on the wider road and continue to drop steeply down the hill. Take care for although this is a narrow country lane it does carry an amount of traffic.

Quite soon the road sweeps left and you pass an old lake on your right which is home to a large number of ducks and coots. Continue to follow the road, with a small brook on your right, to pass Steanbridge Mill which has long since been converted into a luxury house. This valley, like so many valleys which feed their waters into Stroud, was once extremely important for its prolific number of mills and the high quality of the water.

The road now climbs steeply uphill and you need to stop frequently and admire lovely open views that lie below you. Towards the top of the hill you pass Springbank Stables on your right and continue to climb for a further 200 yards.

Now look for a gravel track going off to your left marked by a footpath sign. Walk down the track for a further 150 yards and when the track divides, follow it as it sweeps to the right. Above you and to your right is a large circle of trees.

Quite soon you pass an isolated house on your left and the path peters out. Continue to walk straight ahead, into the field and keep close to the fence on your left. The path now becomes very difficult to follow and you need to walk close to the fence and enter woods in left hand corner.

As you enter the wood the path once again becomes quite obvious and the walking is easy as you begin to drop downhill. After 300 yards as you approach a lake, look out for a path to left, take path and follow the path steeply downhill with Lake on your right.

Follow the path as it meanders through the wood and starts to once again climb quite steeply. At the top of the slope you meet a broad track where you turn left. Stay on this track as it climbs through the wood to finally leave it by a metal gate.

Continue to follow the track which suddenly comes out onto the B4070 which you need to cross with great care. Turn left and follow the grassy verge for a further 200 yards back to Bulls Cross and your car.

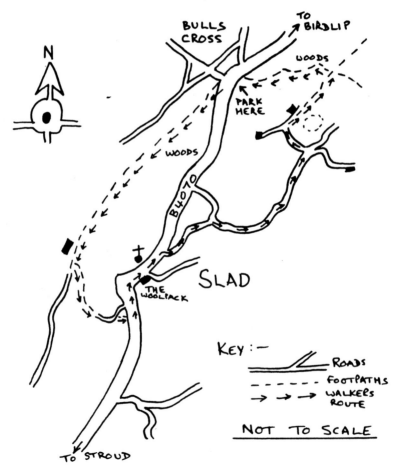

Walk 4 Chedworth to the Roman Villa

Distance: 4 miles Allow: 2 hours

"A stroll through history, across open farmland and through interesting woodlands. Beginning and ending at one of Gloucestershire's best loved pubs, it is a most pleasant walk, whatever the weather."

The walk starts in the heart of Chedworth village, outside the village pub, the "Seven Tuns Inn", which dates back to 1610. This is a "free house" praised for its extensive menu and offering a fine range of "real ales" either at the beginning or end of your journey, or indeed both!

From the inn, cross over the minor road and walk up the narrow footpath towards the church above you. As you do so you will find yourself in a truly rural setting surrounded by picturesque Cotswold stone cottages which appear to glow golden in the sunlight.

At the top of the short climb, join a minor road and turn right to pass the church on your left. After 200 yards, at a 'Y' junction, there is a metal sign on your left pointing you in the direction of the Roman Villa, as you take the left hand fork into a no through road.

When the road ends, go over the stile and follow the yellow arrow sign taking you slightly left around the field and away from the village, keeping a dry stone wall on your left. The wall quickly peters out and you now head across the field to the right hand corner of a small copse, where the footpath takes you over another stile.

Stop and catch your breath before crossing this stile and take your time to look back over your shoulder at a splendid view across Chedworth village.

Now walk up through the copse on a carefully constructed flight of wooden steps. At the top, the path divides and you ignore the path going off to your right and continue straight ahead for 50 yards before going through a small metal gate.

Once again the way divides and you ignore the blue arrowed bridle way crossing your path and follow the yellow arrow sign straight ahead, keeping the dry stone wall on your right. After 300 yards the path across the field takes you over another stile and into a wood and straight on.

Follow the broad and pleasant track through the mature woodland and your way is confirmed, after a short distance, by another metal sign indicating the direction of the Roman Villa. After a further 100 yards the path divides and your way is unmarked. Ignore the track sweeping off to your left and remain on the path that takes you straight ahead.

After 300 yards the path divides four ways and is once again well marked. Take the path to your right marked yet again with an arrow taking you downhill, towards the Roman Villa. You soon pass under an old railway bridge and after a further 200 yards arrive at your destination, the National Trust property, Chedworth Roman Villa.

Enjoying a delightful setting in this peaceful section of the lush Coln valley, the villa was discovered in 1864 when a local man was digging his ferret out of a rabbit hole he had got himself enthusiastically stuck in. Today the remains, which are regarded as some of the finest in Britain, attract vast numbers of visitors each year.

Two old Roman tools to be found in the Roman Villa Museum.
On the left is Iron Shears and on the right is an Iron Mattock, minus its wooden handle.

From the villa continue to walk down the road, taking time to enjoy the lovely view to your left along the valley basin where the River Coln carves a crazy path and paints the prettiest of pictures. Take care walking down this short section of road as it can get quite busy at times with traffic going up and down to the Roman Villa.

At the bottom of the road, at a 'Y' junction, leave the road and take a well marked path going off to your right, passing through the green gates. This is marked as a private road but is a public footpath where the walking is flat and easy for more than a mile and offers really splendid views across the valley.

Here you have the river for company and can often see a myriad of wildlife, whose home is along the riverbank, on this distant corner of the Stowell Park Estate.

At the end of the river walk, the path leaves the estate as you join a minor road and continue straight ahead for about 30 yards before leaving the road. Turn right to cross a stile in the wall onto a well marked footpath, leading up into mature woodland.

The path now climbs quite steeply through the wood and is occasionally confirmed by yellow arrow signs as it eventually flattens out join a major track for 20yds before leaving track and following yellow arrows down into the woodland valley. Follow the main track through the bowl of the wood until it once again climbs out to leave the trees, where a notice declares "Private gallops-keep off".

At this point walk slightly left across the field towards a post where a footpath sign awaits you. The yellow arrow directs you to the lone tree on the horizon where another post tells you that the path divides. Ignore the path straight ahead and turn sharp right to follow the path straight through the centre of the field.

As you follow this path take your time to stop and look around at the fine views behind you over Stowell Park and beyond that, parts of Wiltshire and the Thames Valley.

The path takes you over a large stone stile at the far side of the field and continues straight on over the next field. Pass a lone tree and make your way towards a hedge which you now keep on your left and have a farm fence on your right.

Go through an old farm and straight on, you now have a dry stone wall on your left. This is just about the highest point on your walk and you have unrestricted views in all directions.

Soon the path divides four ways and you take the second blue arrowed path, straight ahead along the lane, with the dry stone wall on your left. Here you have some fine views over Chedworth village and an impressive family home just below you on the left.

When the wall ends, go through a small wooden gate where you leave the bridle way and turn left to go through the metal gate you passed through earlier. Now you arrive at the small copse and retrace your path down the wooden steps taking you back towards Chedworth and your starting point at the "Seven Tuns Inn".

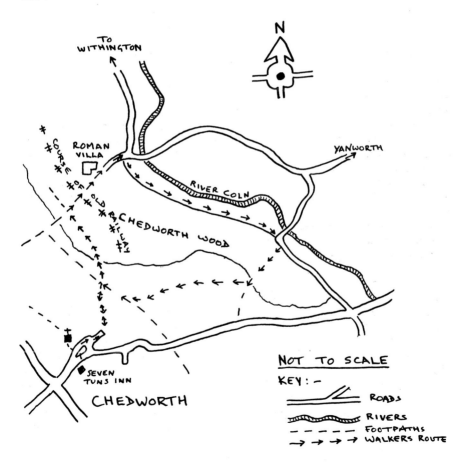

WALK 5 Cold Aston to Notgrove

Distance: 5 miles: Allow: 2 [1/2] hours

"A flat and easy walk around three little known villages with an opportunity to call in at a truly old pub at the beginning and the end. This a very different walk and a real treat."

The walk begins near the green in the centre of the pretty little Cotswold village of Cold Aston outside the "Plough Inn". The pub is a "free house" offering a range of "real ales" and an extensive menu. Dominating the green is a large sycamore tree which lends its name to the handsome Georgian house, Sycamore House, which is close by.

From the inn follow a public footpath sign up the narrow road, passing the inn on your right. After a short walk the road peters out and you continue straight ahead on a narrow path following signs for the "Macmillan Way" and soon cross a stone stile, keeping a dry stone wall on your right.

The path heads towards open fields and you now cross a wooden stile into the field. Here the path divides and you turn right and now have a fence on your right. The path takes you over a large stone stile where you again go straight on. Already there are open views in all directions over fertile fields, dotted with a variety of trees.

Leave this field in the far right hand corner over a third stone stile and here you join a minor country road which you follow to your left. The walking is very easy as the road begins to slope gently down. Off to your left you can catch glimpses of the old Roman Road the Foss Way, now simply called the A429.

When the road dips you pass Bang Up Farm on your right and continue along the road on this easy section. In the distance there is a continuous hum of traffic yet you already have the feeling of being deep in the heart of the country.

After about a mile the track again dips down into a second valley which is very attractive and you are now in a natural bowl. Go through a metal farm gate and continue along the track as it begins to gently rise and sweep around to the right. This is a particularly peaceful section as you walk through a deep, lush and ancient valley, very reminiscent of "downs" country.

As the track leaves the open fields and enters an avenue of trees take your time to stop and admire the view behind you over Cold Aston and the fields all around. There is a variety of colours making up this landscape, dominated by shades of brown, green and blue, like paint blobs on an artists palette, all waiting to be mixed.

As the track begins to dip down you get your first views of the village of Turkdean spread out before you and new views of a pleasant pastoral scene open up to your left.

When you enter Turkdean, at the 'Y' junction turn right. However if you wish to see the village you need to divert to your left and then return to this point.

You now follow the wide country road for two miles. The views it offers make the journey worthwhile but you do need to exercise great care as the road is a popular short cut for local traffic.

You now have new views to your left over the villages of Hazleton and neighbouring Salperton and in the far distance the busy A40 Cheltenham to Oxford road.

After two miles of walking along the ridge and just after passing a set of large iron gates to the local manor house, take the first turning right for Notgrove village and walk under a wonderful avenue of trees.

The Norman church at Notgrove contains a monument to members of the Whittington family, the descendants of Sir Richard (Dick) Whittington and you may choose to visit it before carrying on with the walk. If you do go straight on to the church and then return to this point.

At the junction turn left and follow the road down into the village to pass the telephone kiosk on your left. After passing a small row of cottages, immediately take the minor road off to your right and after a further 300 yards pass a cottage on your left. At this point the road sweeps around to your right and you leave it to continue straight ahead through a farm gate.

"Plough Inn"

You are now on a well marked and well used public footpath taking you off at a sharp left angle across the field and you are heading for a farm gate in the top right hand corner of the field. Go through the gate and follow the direction indicated by a blue arrow to your right along a broad farm track.

After 50 yards leave the track by turning left through a small wooden gate and follow the arrow marker through a wonderful avenue of tall, healthy trees. This is a scene straight off a calendar and your journey along this short section is often accompanied by a continuous chatter of a variety of birds.

Make this most of this last peaceful, country stroll before following the path out of the trees and onto another minor road. Here you turn right and follow the road back into Cold Aston to complete you journey. However the village boasts a fine Norman church which you pass on your left as you return to the green and visiting it makes a pleasant diversion.

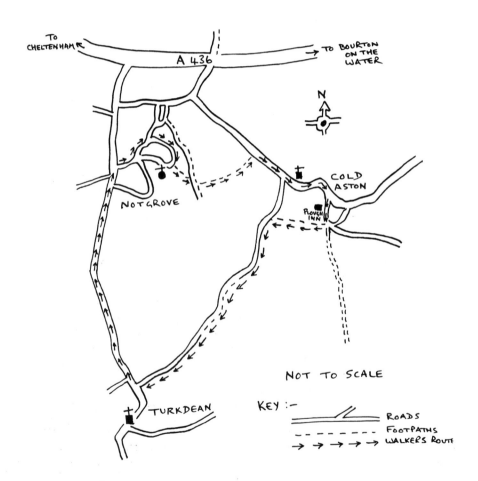

WALK 6 Cranham to Cooper's Hill

Distance: 3 miles Allow: 2 hours

"A breathtaking walk through thick woodland, beginning and ending in one of Gloucestershire's hidden villages. With a well marked track and a resting spot with stunning views, the walk is a true delight."

The walk begins and ends at the "Black Horse" pub in the centre of Cranham. Whether you choose to visit it before you start or on your return, you will not be disappointed as it is a traditional pub offering a variety of "real ales" and boasts a menu that truly caters for all tastes.

Leave the pub and turn right to drop down the narrow road, passing Cranham House on your right. At the 'T' junction cross straight over the road and take a well marked footpath alongside a house called Brookside.

The track drops steeply downhill where you cross a small stream over a series of stepping stones. This is a pretty little spot and offers you a chance to catch your breath before climbing up the path into the wood ahead.

The path soon joins a second path where you turn left and continue to climb the hill. Almost at the top of the climb your track joins a cross roads of paths and you follow the painted yellow and red arrow signs straight ahead. You are walking on a well used path through a variety of trees in the most pleasant woodland imaginable.

Towards the top of the climb the path meets a broad track coming in from your left. Continue to climb for a further 10 yards and then leave the broad track, taking the footpath going off to your left, following the yellow and red arrow. After a further 15 yards the path once again divides and you continue straight ahead, up the slope, ignoring the path going off to your left. As you climb the hill your way is once again confirmed by a yellow and red arrow sign painted on a tree.

At the top of the slope the footpath meets a minor country road where you turn left and pass a house called Buckholt Wood on your right. After 15 yards leave the road and turn right, into the wood.

The path immediately divides and you take the broad track going off to your left, ignoring the path alongside the house. At the top of the track the path goes off to the right, passing a sign welcoming you to "Buckholt Wood" and informing you that "Buckholt is a Saxon word for Beechwood and during the 12th century the wood was a hunting preserve owned by the monks of Gloucester Abbey".

Pass alongside the metal farm gate and again the path divides in three directions. Take the broad centre track straight ahead where once again you pick up the painted yellow red arrow signs. Take your time climbing this section as the woods offer a fine canopy and are a very peaceful home to a variety of wild life.

Near the top of the slope you need to take care as the arrowed track goes off to your right, and you must leave it and continue straight ahead on a broad track, (if you start to descend you have missed the turn). The track soon takes you to another notice, this time welcoming you to "Coopers Hill Nature Reserve".

Pass the sign and in 20yds turn right onto a muddy track. The track broadens and becomes easy walking, and very soon takes you to the view point at the top of Cooper's Hill.

If you hove come equipped for a picnic this is the place to sit and drink in the views. This is the starting line for the annual "Cheese Rolling" and looks out over a panorama stretching from Wales to Worcester.

The Urban sprawl that is Gloucester and Cheltenham competes for attention against nature's hilly backdrop. Laid out like a living map before you are the Black Mountains of South Wales. May Hill with its distinctive trees, Elgar's Malvern Hills, Churchdown, Bredon Hills and Cleeve Cloud with its Radio masts.

When you tire of the views leave the viewpoint by following the "Cotswold Way" signs. The Way divides at this point. Do not go down the hill, but follow the path behind you. which is flat and takes you back into the woods.

Your path is now marked with a Yellow and Orange Arrow, together with the "Cotswold Way" signs. After 200yds at a junction in the paths, turn left along a broad track, still following the Yellow and Orange arrows. Eventually you will pass through a "Pinch Stile", where you turn acute left. passing a Gloucestershire Wildlife Sign. Follow the top path along the edge of the woods, still following the Yellow and Orange arrows.

You are now walking parallel to the A46, Cheltenham to Stroud road. Ignore the Yellow and Orange arrows that point right down wooden steps (these lead to a Car Park), and continue to follow the Yellow and Orange arrows pointing ahead.

The path turns left and climbs steeply. At the top of the hill at the "Buckholt Wood" sign. the Cotswold Way turns right, but you carry on straight, following the Yellow and Orange arrows.

The track is broad and the walking is both downhill and easy. Very soon you again come to a minor country road, which you need to cross straight over with care. As you enter this section of woodland the path divides three ways and you take the left hand path and once again pick up the Yellow and Orange arrows. The path continues downhill and after 30yds bears right.

As you enter this section of woodland the path divides three ways and you take the left hand path and once again pick up the Yellow and Orange arrows. The path continues downhill and after 30yds bears right.

The track eventually emerges onto another country road, close to the sign for Cranham village. Here you turn left and carefully follow the road back into the village, re-tracing your steps to the "Black Horse" pub for a celebratory drink.

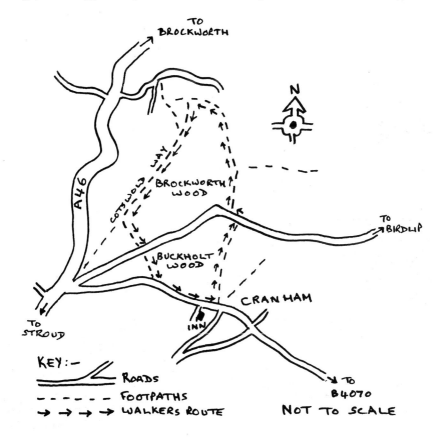

WALK 7 Crickley Hill Country Park

Distance: 2 miles Allow: 1[1/2] hours

"A stroll around this popular site, beginning and ending in the visitors' carpark. With a varied landscape offering outstanding views and a real ale pub for a rest, this is a pleasant,easy walk,to be savoured time and time again."

Follow the service road into Crickley Hill Country Park from its entrance off the B4070 Cheltenham to Birdlip road. Park you car in the top carpark which is on your right, just before the Visitors' Information Centre. This is the start and end of the short walk.

Parts of Crickley Hill are scheduled as "An Ancient Monument" and you will be treading in the footsteps of people who have made their home here for more than 5,000 years. The Park is nationally important for its geology and rock formations and offers sanctuary to a wide variety of birds, animals and insects in its extensive, lush woodland. The site is cared for in partnership by Gloucestershire County Council and the National Trust through the ever watchful eyes of the "Cotswold Volunteer Wardens' Service".

Walk through the carpark,away from the Information Centre on the trail of the "Cotswold Way". Climb a small flight of steps and within 10 yards you meet a wide track and turn left to follow the track downhill.

As the track sweeps left the views ahead and around you begin to open up and set before you are the most magnificent sights that this part of the county has to offer. To your left you look deep into Wales and glimpse its mountain ranges, ending at Hay Bluff. Ahead are the Malvern Hills and to your right Cleeve Common and Leckhampton Hill. Below is a wide and deep basin offering shelter to the urban areas of Cheltenham and Gloucester.

Ignore any paths going off right or left and continue to follow the stony track as it steeply descends. You cross over several marked paths as you complete this walk and very soon you pass a yellow arrow sign on your right bearing the number three.

Close to the bottom of the slope, with the large wooden gate about 100 yards away, leave the path and take the track going off to your left, again marked by a yellow arrow. Now stay on the well marked and well used path as it slowly makes its way uphill passing posts numbered four, five and six. At the top of the climb and at a series of wooden steps, at "T" Junction turn left and make your way to the viewpoint.

Now keep the dry stone wall close on your right for some considerable distance. The walking is flat and very easy after the climb and as you catch you breath you have the opportunity to admire fresh views out towards Birdlip and Painswick.

Go through a wooden gate and continue straight ahead, still with the wall on your right. You are heading for the wood ahead of you, known as "The Scrubs" and you are once again following the distinctive "Cotswold Way" signs. The path threads its way through dense woodland and as you emerge from the trees you have a wooden fence on your right and you are close to the A417 road.

Stay close to the fence and make your way to the far right hand corner of the field and follow the path through a small wooden gate and up to the main road. Your resting point at the "Air Balloon" pub lies opposite you across the busy road. Cross it with great care.

The "Air Balloon" is a fine old pub offering a wide selection of drinks, including a variety of "real ales", and boasts an extensive menu.

To complete the walk, re-cross the A417 and go back through the little wooden gate. Now keep the hedge on your right and make your way towards the green cricket pavilion on your right. Go through the gate and walk straight ahead, keeping the wooden fence on your right.

After 200 yards, cross over the service road and start to follow the new marker signs which start at number three. You are now on a gentle slope and the well marked path goes through another gate on your left and then off at a slight right angle. Again its very easy walking.

This section of woodland is called "Wardens' Wood" and was planted in 1990, sponsored by the locally based ICI Fibres and dedicated to the "Cotswold Volunteer Wardens' Service" to mark its 30th anniversary.

The views have again changed and off to your right is a glimpse of Leckhampton Hill and its famous quarries which supplied much of the stone to build Regency Cheltenham.

At marker number six the path divides. Ignore the path to the left and continue straight ahead and through a gate into the wood. Your way now goes off to the left,threading through the trees to eventually pick up the yellow arrow signs marking the "Cotswold Way".

Follow the signs out of the wood, across the green pasture land, through a final "kissing gate" and back to your car.

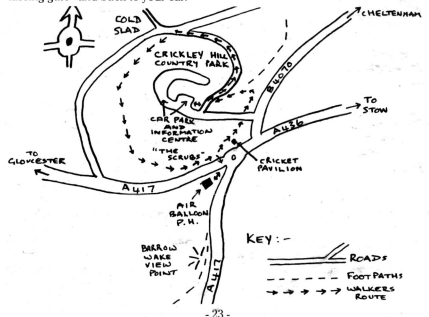

WALK 8 Great Rissington along the Windrush

Distance: 3 miles Allow: 2 hours

"A flat stroll through open farmland, beginning and ending at one of the prettiest of pubs. A chance to stroll along a Cotswold river and admire village cottages almost forgotten by time."

This walk is best enjoyed in the summer months and you need appropriate footwear in other seasons as it can get quite muddy.

Park your car near the village green in Great Rissington and start your journey from the "Lamb Inn", a "free house", which you can visit either before you start or on your return. The pub offers a wide choice of beers, including "real ales", and boasts an extensive menu.

From the pub walk down into the village, keeping the green on your left, following the signs to the church, passing the telephone kiosk on your left.

Great Rissington is a truly old village with a variety of tastefully restored houses,most of which are built from the local "Cotswold" stone. The village is spread along the Windrush valley and many of the cottage gardens face westward for the fine views.

Walk down to the church and as you approach it take time to admire the magnificent building to its left which is the Manor House and encapsulates everything that is truly "Cotswold". The church itself is well worth visiting. It is the Church of St.John the Baptist,a Norman church, parts of which date back to 1200. It boasts a fine 15th century tower with pinnacles and battlements. Within the tower are six 18th century bells from the famous Rudhall foundry in Gloucester.

Returning from the churchyard turn right and follow an arrow sign towards the Windrush Agricultural Estates and enter an area marked as a "Private Road" where a series of old farm barns have been tastefully converted into fine houses. After passing Drovers Barn on your right, turn right and follow the yellow arrow signs through a garden.

Cross a gate and continue down the driveway, taking time to admire the fine views ahead of you. Just before the next sign which indicates "Private Road - No Entry", turn left on a well used footpath which now takes you diagonally across the field.

The path takes you down to the bottom left hand corner of the field where you cross a ditch and turn right, keeping the ditch on your right. After 100 yards turn left to follow the footpath at a sharp angle across the field.

At the far side of this field turn right, keeping another ditch on your left. At the bottom of this field go through a gate and turn left where the path threads its way through a sparse wood,again keeping the hedge on your left. You are now deep into the country with no buildings in sight and it is a very peaceful place.

Soon you are joined on your walk by the fast flowing River Windrush on your right and you follow it on its journey to the River Thames. The river is wide and shallow at this point and home to a variety of wildlife including ducks, swans and coots.

At the end of the wooded section cross a gate and wooden bridge and continue straight ahead. The path is well used and cared for and winds its way through the trees and bushes, heading to your left. When you break free from the trees and enter a field turn right and keep the hedge on your right. The track now follows the field as it sweeps round left until you almost complete a half circle where the arrows take your right, and over a ditch.

Once again turn right and keep the river on your right as you make your way around the field, and at the end of the field exit to your right. In 20yds at the Bridle Way, turn left, going up hill on a gravel path with the woods on your right. At the end of the woods the paths turns to grass and bends first to the left and then to the right.

Near the top of the hill, just before a circular clump of trees, follow the Blue arrows to your left and cross the field. This is a good place to stop and admire the fine views around and behind you. In the valley below are the villages of Windrush and Sherbourne looking for all the world like the model village at Bourton on the Water. Beyond them is the busy A40 Cheltenham to Oxford road with its constant lines of traffic.

Pass through the gate and cross diagonally right across the field. You then reach a large track, turn left and continue along the track for 1/2 mile as you make your way back into Great Rissington. The track eventually meets a metalled, village road where you turn right to make your way back to the "Lamb Inn" and your car.

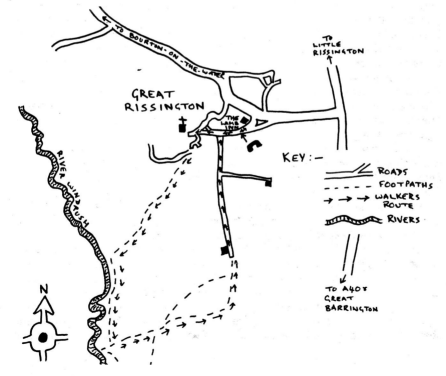

WALK 9 Guiting Power to Kineton

Distance: 4[1/2] miles Allow: 2[1/2] hours

"A gentle stroll through open farmland, beginning and ending in one of Gloucestershire's prettiest villages. With a varied landscape and two or three pubs for a rest, this is a delightful walk."

Snacks and provisions for this walk should not be a problem, as it starts and ends at the "Farmers Arms" pub, just below the stone cross in the centre of Guiting Power, close to the village Post Office and Watsons Bakery. The stroll passes three pubs in all, two selling the famous "Donnington real ale" and the other being a "free house", with character in abundance.

The golden coloured cottages which make up this splendid village give it a unique balance and are irresistible to any keen photographer as Guiting Power shouts out "Cotswolds".

Leave the "Farmers Arms" and walk through the village in the direction of Winchcombe, passing the cross on your left and the Post Office on your right. Take the first turning right into a narrow road which is a "no through road". Signed Wardens Way, Bus Turning Bay. The way is bordered by some tastefully restored cottages and beyond is the pleasing sight of open, lush fields.

When the road peters out, go through a metal gate and continue straight on, down a well used footpath, which gradually descends to the valley below. You are following the "Wardens' Way" and will stay on it for about a mile, until you arrive at Guiting Wood.

At the bottom of the slope, the path divides at a small river; do not cross the river but continue to follow the path straight ahead, now rising out of the valley basin through mature woodland. When you have passed a large barn on your left, turn right onto a wide farm track, following the Wardens way signs with its charactic "W".

The walking is both flat and easy and the views most rewarding. Ahead is Guiting Wood and off to the right an open aspect of rolling farm land at Castlett and Barton. Soon the Manor House itself comes into view and, whatever the season, never fails to please the eye.

The broad track eventually takes you through a metal farm gate and begins to rise quite steadily. At the top of the rise the path divides and you cross the junction to continue straight ahead, with the Manor House on your left. The views of the house are now unrestricted and quite glorious. Here you leave the Wardens way.

Follow the narrow road as it eventually sweeps around to the right and you pass a little cottage on your left. Go through the wooden farm gate and stay on the road as it enters Castlett Wood and walk through an avenue of trees; this is a conservation area.

As the road dips down, the wood begins to close in on you and forms a natural canopy above your head. The walking remains very easy and most pleasant and you now have a little stream in the valley to your right for company.

After half a mile you come to a wooden fence on your right and just beyond it an old mill pool. Here you turn right, through a gap in the fence, onto an unmarked bridle way with the pool immediately on your left. This little used path, which can get quite muddy, now steadily climbs the hillside.

The path eventually bursts out from the trees and passes between open fields before broadening. You are now level with the tree tops and new, more stunning views lay around and below you.

At the top of the lane is a large boulder which has been lovingly carved into the likeness of a massive toad with a snake on its back. This is the handiwork of an itinerant artist who passes through the "Cotswolds" each year painting pub signs and the like or simply carving stones, as the fancy takes him.

At the junction turn right onto a wide, stony track and begin to climb the steady slope. Soon new views open up and off to the right you can see the Norman tower of Guiting Power Parish Church forcing its way up through the trees.

The walking remains very easy and all the while new views open up around you. Soon, to your left, the church tower at Temple Guiting comes into view, close to the famous Cotswold Llama Farm.

Llama

As the track begins to slowly descend you get your first glimpse of the half way point at Kineton and you chance to stop at the village pub.

The track sweeps around to the right and joins a metalled road. Here turn left and walk down the road with care to a 'Y' junction where you turn right, following a sign for Guiting Power. Very soon you arrive at the Donnington pub, aptly named the "Half Way House".

Like all the 15 Donnington pubs this one offers a range of their popular "real ales" and is gaining a reputation for fine quality meals and snacks.

From the pub, continue to walk out of the village towards Guiting Power and after the last building on the left turn right through a farm gate towards a large, open farm barn. You are walking on a public footpath with barn on your right.

The path now gently rises and you need to keep the dry stone wall on your left. Soon the wall gives way to a hedge on your left. At the end of the field and just before a wooden gate go left through a gap in the hedge, then turn immediately right and cross a wooden stile.

Walk straight down the field, keeping the fence and hedge on your left. The views again open up to your right and you are once more treated to a fine view of Guiting Manor and its surrounding woodland.

In the bottom left hand corner of the field go over three stiles, through the garden of a house to join a minor road, here you turn right and walk along the road.

At the 'T' junction turn left and follow the narrow road steeply downhill to a ford which you cross on a footbridge. Now climb up the other side to pass through the metal gate of this gated road.

After 50 yards, at the crossroads, turn left onto the broad stony track that you followed earlier. When the track ends, opposite the bungalow, turn right and follow the road up the hill.

At the 'Y' junction turn left and carefully make your way back into the village of Guiting Power. Very soon you arrive at the second of the two village pubs, "Ye Olde Inne", which is a "free house", popular for both its ales and food.

Continue to follow the road into the village centre, drinking in the sight of the lovely old cottages along the way. Very soon you arrive at the village cross which you now pass on your right as you make your way back to the "Farmers Arms" to complete your journey.

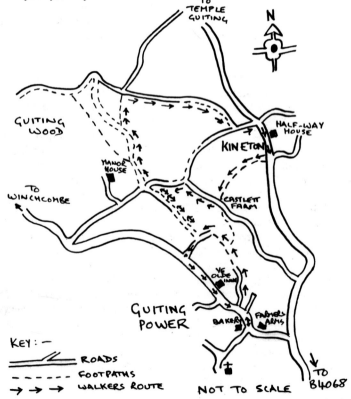

Walk 10 - Kilkenny to Pegglesworth

Distance: 4 miles Allow: 2 hours

"A strikingly different walk through woods and open farmland. Another opportunity to take in some of Gloucestershire's finest views with a traditional country pub to complete the perfect day."

Park the car at the Kilkenny Viewpoint Car Park off the A436 Gloucester to Andoversford road, which is about 300 yards from today's pub, the "Kilkenny Inn". This walk can be muddy in parts so you should come prepared.

From the car park, walk away from the main road across the rough ground in the direction of the radio mast at the top of the hill. Here you leave the field via a "kissing gate" and join a metalled road, where you turn left to continue uphill. Although this is a minor country road it is well used by local traffic and you need to take care.

On a clear day the views along the road continue to open up and change. Behind you are the wooded slopes of Dowdeswell and very soon, to your left, the lush pastures surrounding Shipton Oliffe and out to Cleeve Hill and beyond.

On your left on the crest of the hill are the remains of an ancient burial mound topped by larch trees which is known simply by the biblical name of St.Paul's Epistle.

Follow the road as it gently descends and passes through an avenue of small trees. Very soon you leave the road by turning right onto a well used track signposted as a 'Public Bridleway' and opposite Foxcote Hill House. This is a gated track with a good walking surface and soon offers pleasant country views in all directions. The walking is very easy and should not be rushed.

Having passed the cottage, follow the track as it sweeps around to your left, keeping the large trees on your right. The way is now marked with a blue arrow sign. It is quite common to be accompanied along the way by a variety of wildlife such as partridge and pheasant as well as a selection of farm stock.

The track eventually sweeps around to the left towards some old barns and having passed these, turn right onto the farm road. Again take time to admire the fine old Cotswold stone built Pegglesworth House.

Now follow the road towards the cottages in the distance and at the 'Y' junction, continue to follow the road to the left still marked with white arrow signs. At the end of the driveway cross the busy A436 with care and follow a footpath sign away from the road, with a dry stone wall on your right.

Very soon the path divides. Ignore the path going off to your right and continue straight ahead to pass a "squeeze stile". The path first goes left and then once again divides; here you follow the path taking you steeply downhill on a series of wooden steps deep into Lineover Wood.

"Lineover", after which the wood is named means, "lime bank" in Anglo Saxon. The area, which is now cared for by the Woodland Trust, is 111 acres in size and was first recorded around 800 A.D.

At the bottom of the long slope go over a wooden stile and continue down a small flight of wooden steps into a field. Once again there are fine views down over Dowdeswell and left towards Cheltenham. The path now snakes its way through a small copse and you need to walk to the centre of the field before turning sharp right towards a small fingerpost (Cotswold Way).

Pass the house on your left and continue to make your way downhill towards the gate ahead of you to re-enter the dense woodland. You are now following signs bearing a black acorn with a white dot which signifies that you are on the "Cotswold Way".

The main track again snakes its way through these lovely old woods and you should ignore any minor paths going off to the right or left.

Leave the wood still following the "Cotswold Way" signs, heading slightly left across the field. After 100 yards you need to take great care as the path divides. However it is only the Cotswold Way which is marked to your left and the path that you now need to follow goes to your right, across the field. Ignore the kissing gate and turn right to head for the far right hand corner of the field ahead of you to pass between the two telegraph posts in the field.

Here the path again divides and is only partly marked. Ignore the path going straight ahead and turn left to join a track taking you around the hillside towards a large farm barn in the valley. This track is not marked.

The views are at their best along this stretch and should be savoured. On a clear day the deep valley off to your left offers fine views of woods and fields, the colours changing with the seasons.

Go through the large metal farm gate to the right of the barn and continue to walk straight ahead, passing a further two barns on your left. The way now goes through a second gate and takes you away from the buildings along a farm road, with a dry stone wall on your right.

The walking is again very easy and continues to offer fine country views and open fields along the way. On your left is the site of an Iron Age settlement but little remains to identify it today.

After a further half mile there is a footpath sign leaving the road to the right. If you wish to cut short your walk then turn right here and climb the slope back to the car park. However if you wish to visit the pub, keep straight ahead and follow the road into the hamlet of Upper Dowdeswell.

Here you pass between a series of Cotswold stone cottages and an old water hole, which dates back to the 1870's, on your right. At the 'T' junction turn right and walk carefully up the narrow road to the "Kilkenny Inn", on your left at the next junction.

The "Kilkenny Inn" is a "free house" offering a fine selection of "real ales" and boasts an extensive menu to cater for all tastes.

On leaving the pub, carefully cross the busy A436 and turn right to follow the verge back in the direction of Gloucester. The view point and car park are just a short walk along the road and off to your left.

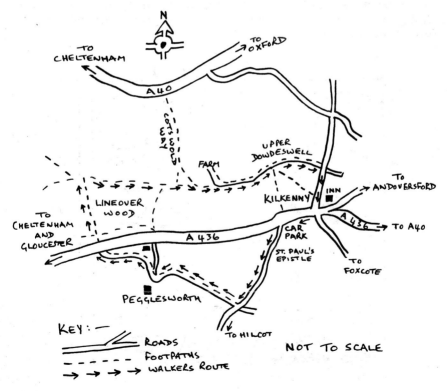

Walk 11 - Laverton to Stanton

Distance: 3 miles Allow: 2 hours

"A challenging walk with a hilly start, rewarded with outstanding views deep into both Gloucestershire and neighbouring Worcestershire, with a chance to stop and rest at a real ale pub in a traditional Cotswold village."

The walk starts in the centre of Laverton,a pretty little village just off the B4632, Winchcombe to Broadway road, where you can leave your car in the wide street,close to the Post Office.

Walk out of the village towards hills. The road soon peters out and becomes a track as you pass Orchard Barn on your right. Go through an old wooden gate and straight ahead on a well used path.

The going soon gets tough as the path climbs steeply uphill with a small brook on your right. Try to find frequent excuses to stop and catch your breath on this section and look back at the magnificent views opening up behind you. Already you have a panoramic view over Broadway, out towards Evesham and across the valley to Bredon Hill.

The path is not well marked with the exception of a solitary orange arrow encouraging you to keep climbing. This is the only climb of the walk and you will very soon be rewarded for it.

Almost at the top of the slope fine views open up ahead and to the left of you, crowned by the sight of Broadway Tower. This folly was built by the Earl of Coventry for his wife and looks down on the town and the surrounding counties. Behind you the view includes the peaks of the "Malvern Hills".

The path has now become a wide dirt track which very soon joins a second track at a 'T' junction. This is the "Cotswold Way" and you join it by turning to your right. The walking is now easy with just a gentle slope and the views continue to expand. Clearly visible off to your right is the tree-topped May Hill and beyond it the Black Mountains and Wales.

The track is marked by a yellow arrow sign indicating the "Cotswold Way" beginning its long journey down to Bath. Do not take the path off to your right which is opposite an old metal barn but continue straight ahead for another half mile and you now have a fine view of Snowshill village to your left and to your right Nottingham Hill and Cleeve Common.

As the track draws to an end at a junction of tracks, leave the "Cotswold Way" as it continues straight ahead and turn right on a broad track around the curve of the field. After a further 40 yards go through a metal gate.

You now begin to quickly descend the hill with its breathtaking views over much of the county and far beyond. The path is stony and can at certain times of the year become quite muddy at its base.

Go through another metal gate and continue down the slope and into the village of Stanton. Almost immediately you arrive at its popular pub, "The Mount". This is one of the 15 "Donnington" pubs on the Cotswolds and offers their famous range of "real ales" in addition to fine selection of meals.

This is your reward for the earlier climb. The pub and its beer garden command a wonderful view over the village and far beyond to Dumbleton Hill, Bredon Hill, the Malvern Hills and the Cleeve Hill escarpment.

From "The Mount" continue downhill to the village and a chance to step back in time as you pass between a row of lovely old houses, many of which date back to the 17th century. Stanton owes much of its glory to Sir Philip Stott, an architect who bought the estate in 1906 and spent the next 30 years in restoration work.

At the fine old stone cross, outside Cross Cottage, turn right and walk down to St. Michael's church, entering the churchyard through its wooden gate. Turn right again and pass to the right side of the building, following a yellow arrow sign with a black dot.

Leave the churchyard in the far right hand corner and follow the path between two high walls. At the end of this short section do not go over the stile ahead of you but follow the path to the left, keeping the iron fence and hedge on your left. Go through a large metal "kissing gate", turn right to cross a small wooden bridge and turn left. Now walk straight ahead, down the field.

Cross a stile and turn right to keep the hedge on your right. The path is well used and marked by a yellow arrow sign with a black dot as it continues straight ahead over a series of fields and stiles. To your right are fine views of your earlier journey and although you are walking parallel with the busy B4632 road it feels as though you are deep in the countryside.

All too soon you leave the fields and emerge onto a metalled road where you turn right to re-enter the village of Laverton. The road loops around to your left through an architectural mixture of houses which eventually leads you back to the centre and your car.

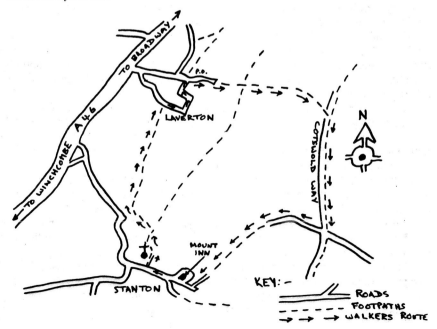

Walk 12 - Northleach to Eastington

Distance: 4 miles Allow: 2 hours

"A very different walk through lush countryside with an infant Cotswold river for company. The walk starts and ends in an old "wool" town, well stocked with tea shops, hotels and pubs. This is easy walking in an area renowned for its beauty."

Park your car in the market place right in the heart of Northleach where you will find a good selection of shops and pubs to set you on your way and greet you again on your return.

"Sherborne Arms"

Northleach is a fine old "wool" town which got its name from the mere fact that it was built just north of the River Leach. Built on the wealth of the wool trade, it boasts a magnificent 15th century church which dominates the town centre and is well worth a visit before you set off.

From the "Sherborne Arms" in the market place walk into High Street and turn right at the Cotswold Stores. Very soon you pass on your left the award winning museum, Keith Harding's World of Mechanical Music. This features antique clocks, musical boxes, automata and mechanical musical instruments of all kinds and is worth taking time out to visit.

Pass the museum on your left and continue to follow the main road out of the town, enjoying the diversity of architecture as you go. Stay on the pavement alongside the main road, heading towards the busy A40 by-pass, until you come to the de-restriction signs, marking the town boundary.

Here you leave the road and take a yellow arrowed footpath on your right, through a "kissing gate" and into a field. Now cross the field at a slight left angle and go over a wooden stile, then continue straight ahead.

Soon you meet a minor metalled service road where you turn right onto the road. Cross the infant River Leach and go into the field on your left, through a large metal gate. Keep walking ahead at a slight right angle. Although this section is not marked it is quite easy to follow.

Now head in the direction of a small cottage on the hilltop. The views are good as you walk through a green, lush valley which is well stocked with a variety of trees. Below you the river snakes an erratic path through the valley basin.

Do not go up to the cottage but head for the top right-hand corner the drystone wall ahead and to the left of you. Cross over a large stone stile, adjacent to a water trough using the thoughtfully provided steps. Keep close to the wall on your right as this short section can get quite muddy. Now pass by a small copse and walk straight ahead.

Soon you arrive at the pretty little hamlet of Upper End,which you pass on your right. Now begin to drop downhill to a wooden farm gate in the hedgerow where your path divides. Go through the gate, turn left and drop down towards the river on a wide track.

Cross the footbridge and follow the track uphill to eventually emerge in fields continue forwards keeping the low drystone wall on your left. There are fine views in all directions and the walking again becomes very easy.

When you arrive at a large farm barn, turn right onto a wide farm track and follow it down to a minor country road where you again turn right. Now follow the road downhill into the hidden village of Eastington, where you turn right at the 'T' junction.

The village is a true delight. The valley setting is sprinkled with a variety of cottages and well kept gardens. The whole place is in harmony with the surroundings and it is a pity to rush through here.

Pass the telephone kiosk on your right and continue straight ahead, down a 'No through road'. Wind your way between the houses to pass Yew Tree Cottage and go over a stone stile. Here the path divides. Do not go straight ahead, where the footpath is marked but turn right and drop down the field, heading for a gate in the drystone wall ahead of you. In the direction of large house on hill.

Cross the field and pass the house on your left as you go through two gates. Now continue straight ahead and pass the two farm barns on your left.

At the end of the field the footpath drops down to your right where you go through a large metal gate back onto the track that you left previously. Here you turn right.

After 20 yards go through the wooden gate on your left and retrace your steps to Upper End. Circle around the first house and go through a small gate with post box into the hamlet. Now turn right and follow the road away from the houses.

At the 'T' junction cross straight over the road and join the broad 'Public Path' opposite. Now follow the path for about a quarter of a mile, enjoying the fine views all around including the occasional glimpse of Northleach and its church nestling below you.

When level with the church tower look for a yellow arrowed footpath going off to your right and follow it, keeping the drystone wall on your left.

Continue to follow the direction of the arrows as they take you downhill over a series of fields and stiles.

Eventually the path loops around a small playing area to make its way back into the centre of the town, offering you a second chance to sightsee and quench your thirst.

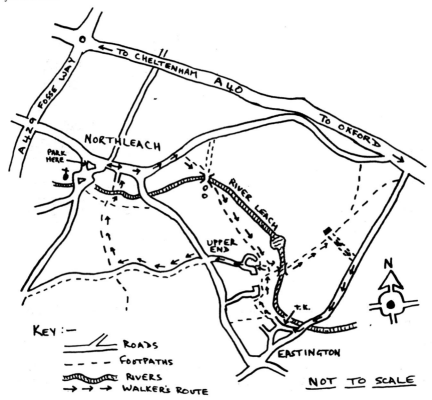

- 36 -

Walk 13 - Painswick to Cranham

Distance: 5 miles Allow: 2[1/2] hours

"Although this is a well known walk for many it is none the worse for that. It starts and ends in one of Gloucestershire's quaintest villages and follows its well turfed golf course to a splendid pub for a rest. This is an easy walk with magnificent views."

Park your car in the Wick Street car park, close to the church in the centre of Painswick, which is just off the A46 Cheltenham to Stroud road.

Walk alongside the main road back in the direction of Cheltenham, passing the famous clipped yew trees and table tombs in the churchyard of St.Mary's Church along with its impressive lychgate. The 15th century church is well worth visiting now or on your return.

Painswick is an old "wool" town firmly established on the Cotswold tourist trail and has its fair quota of pubs, hotels and tea shops, set within its greystone buildings; some of which date back to the 14th century.

"Lychgate"
At the west corner of the Churchyard

Walk up New Street to the traffic lights and turn left into Gloucester Street, following the B4073 road towards Gloucester. At the top of the street, cross the junction with care into Gloucester Road and walk out of the town on the 'B' road. After the last property turn right into Golf Course Road, following the Cotswold Way finger post. This sign signifies that you are walking on the famous "Cotswold Way".

Walk up the road and after 100 yards turn left onto a stony track rambles car park, continuing to climb the steady slope with a small wood on your left. Soon you rejoin the road and turn left and after a further 50 yards turn left again onto a track, once again picking up the Cotswold Way arrows.

After 20 yards turn right and continue to follow the "Cotswold Way" signs as they begin to take you over the fairways of the golf course. Be aware that this is a popular course and there is always a threat from mis-hit golf balls as you follow the route.

You now steadily climb the hill to a Cotswold stone wall which you pass on your right. This is a good time to stop and catch your breath and admire the view behind you.

When the wall ends, safer at this point to cross fairway, at woods opposite, turn left uphill and continue keeping woods on your right, follow woods round to right and continue to viewpoint

From here you have almost unrestricted views in all directions. To your right is the green valley of the aptly named hamlet of Paradise, named by King Charles I who, while bombarding Gloucester, stayed there and described it as the most delightful spot he had ever seen. Ahead is Painswick Beacon and off to your left you look over Gloucester City deep into Worcestershire and the Forest of Dean and the distinctive landmark of May Hill.

Head down the hill, keeping the quarry fence and stone works close to your right. At the bottom of the hill cross the minor metalled road and continue straight ahead, once again picking up the "Cotswold Way" signs. Follow the well used stony path, keeping the trees on your right and the Beacon off to your left.

Eventually the path flattens out and the walking once again becomes very easy with pleasant views off to your right. This is a splendid spot and although you are walking parallel with the A46 you are above it and consequently not bothered by its noise.

The path eventually peters out at the final green of the golf course but you need to continue on until the path meets a very minor road which takes you down to the half way point on the journey, your resting place at the "Royal William". This is a nice old pub which has been restored over the years to become a popular eating house of the "Harvester" chain. The menu is extensive and complemented by a wide range of beers and drinks.

From the pub, retrace your steps back to the golf course to once again follow it back to the "Beacon". This time keep the large wood close to your right and the golf course on your left. You are again on a well trodden stony path and the walking is easy.

Eventually the path begins to rise and you get your first view of the "Trig" point on the summit. Pick any one of the many paths that wind their way across the old hill leading to the "Trig" point.

"Spectacle Stocks" Behind the south east corner of the Churchyard in Painswick

- 38 -

From here you get the most magnificent views of the entire walk. On a clear day you can see Gloucester and Cheltenham spread out like a carpet below you, broken only by the hills at "Robins Wood" and Churchdown. Beyond this are mountains deep into Wales and you can follow the silvery snaking trail of the River Severn as it begins to broaden and pass under the Severn Bridge on its way to the sea. This is a good place to linger a while and just watch the world go by.

Your return journey now takes you off the "Beacon" and back down the slope to the minor road, which you again cross with care. Here you once again pick up the "Cotswold Way" signs and follow them to your left, heading towards Catbrain Quarry.

The "Way" takes you right up to the quarry entrance and then off to the left on a well used, narrow track through the woods. This is a pleasant section spoilt only by the drone of traffic on the busy A46 below.

When the path eventually re-emerges onto the golf course continue to follow the yellow arrow signs across the fairway to retrace your path back into the town.

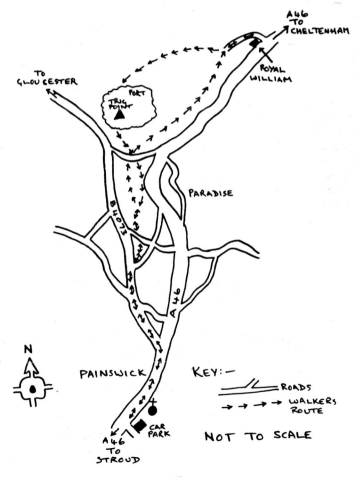

Walk 14 - Seven Springs to Devil's Chimney

Distance: 4 miles Allow: 2 hours

"A glorious stroll through open country,offering some of Gloucestershire's finest views. With a landscape which varies dramatically with the four seasons, this delightful walk is guaranteed to give you an appetite for the pub at the beginning and end."

The walk begins at the lay-by on A436 Andoversford to Gloucester road opposite the "Seven Springs" pub. The pub and its restaurant make a convenient "watering hole" either now or at the end of the walk. Its menu is extensive as is the range of "real ales".

From the lay-by walk up the road, passing the pub on your right, to the junction with the busy A435 Cheltenham to Cirencester road. Here turn left and after 50 yards, left again into the minor road, Hartley Lane. You are now on the old stage coach road and soon get the feeling of being in the country.

After a quarter of a mile, when the road sweeps left, leave it and continue to walk straight ahead on a narrow dirt track; this is Sandy Lane and you are following the sign to Leckhampton Hill (Cotswold Way). The track can get muddy and it is advisable to come prepared with the right footwear.

After a further 300 yards and just past the wettest section the path divides. Here leave the main track and turn left into pastureland and start to climb the incline. The footpath keeps close to the hedge on the left and at the top of the field turns right to once again have a hedge on the left. In the Spring and Summer months this field is rich in a dense carpet of wild flowers.

As you steadily climb the field, fine views open up to your right of Wistley Hill and its common, Vineyards Farm, Ravensgate Hill and down into Cheltenham itself.

The path leaves the field in the top left hand corner and snakes its way through a small copse before breaking out into the open common land which makes up the majority of this walk.

Continue to pick your way along the well walked track, taking care to avoid the prickly gorse bushes. Below you are the lush greens of Lilleybrook Golf Course and all the while the vast panorama continues to open up. The path is still steadily climbing at this point and when it finally flattens out a stout wooden bench offers the excuse to sit and catch you breath and drink in the fine views.

As you once again follow the track, keeping the open aspect on your right, the way is marked by a series of posts bearing an arrow and a black acorn, signifying that you are following the "Cotswold Way".

Your way gently curves around the escarpment to your left and when it arrives at a narrow section, with a farm gate on your left, do not go through the gate but continue to follow the path through a sparse sprinkling of fir trees. The path is once again well marked through this section.

As you break out from these trees you will see just ahead of you the familiar sight of a white painted "Trig" point and your path lies just to the right of this. Now make your way to the edge of the old quarry where there is a topograph marking out the various views that can be seen when the weather permits.

Follow the escarpment around to your left and briefly drop down to the quarry below to enjoy the view from the famous "Devil's Chimney" itself. This solitary column is the creation of the quarry workers in the early 19th century and makes a wonderful photograph on a nice day. It is quite remarkable to think that the coarse ragstone quarried here for 70 years was extracted, transported and delivered for the unaltered cost of one shilling (5p) per 25 cwt.

Now rejoin the path as it continues around the edge of the hill, always keeping the drop on your right. The views now offered on your right include Birdlip Hill, the city of Gloucester, the ever distinctive May Hill and the Black Mountains beyond.

When the path leaves the hill top you pass Salterley Quarry on your right before dropping down to a minor road where you turn left, still following a sign for the "Cotswold Way". Although this is a minor road you need to exercise care as it is well used by local traffic.

Just before you reach a cottage at the top of the hill, the walk leaves the road and goes off to your right. Immediately the path divides and you now leave the "Cotswold Way" trail. It goes off to the right on a well used track and you fork left, into the field, keeping close to the hedge and dry stone wall on your left.

At the end of this field, when the wall peters out, go into the second field and keep walking straight ahead in the same direction, with a large hedge on your left hand side.

REARDON.

The DEVIL'S CHIMNEY.
CHELTENHAM.

When the field comes to an end, cross the wooden stile and begin to descend this field, now going diagonally right. At the bottom, go over a second stile into a narrow field and walk up the deep valley ahead of you through a broad avenue of mature trees. This is a truly delightful section and should not be hurried.

The walk continues along the valley to leave the field over a stile in the top left hand corner. Keep straight ahead with an old iron fence and hedgerow on your left.

Very soon you leave this field, cross a stile and descend to the busy A436 that you left earlier. This is a very dangerous section and the road should be crossed with great care.

Having crossed the road turn left and follow the verge for 20 yards where you leave this unpleasant section of road to turn right into the field on an unmarked footpath. The path drops steadily downhill and you have a mature hedgerow on your left.

Leave the field in the bottom left hand corner by crossing a stile and walk straight ahead with an old fence on your right. The path leaves the field in the bottom right hand corner via a stile and "kissing gate".

You are yet again alongside the busy A436 where you turn right and follow the grassy verge the short distance back to the Seven Springs lay-by and your second chance to visit the pub.

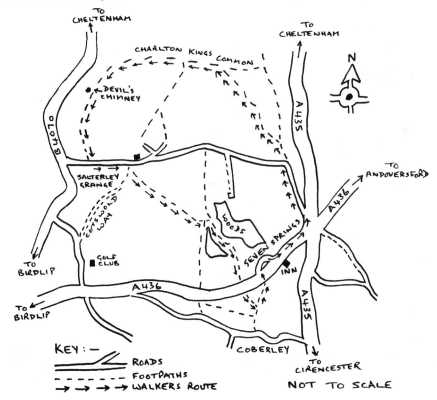

KEY :—
════ ROADS
- - - - - - - FOOTPATHS
→ → → → WALKERS ROUTE

NOT TO SCALE

- 42 -

Walk 15 - Sheepscombe to Overtown

Distance: 4 miles Allow: 2 hours

"An unforgettable stroll through woods and open farmland. It starts and ends in one of the prettiest of villages,and provides two opportunities to visit a pub of traditional style which is guaranteed to offer a warm welcome"

Start the walk by leaving the "Butchers Arms" public house in the centre of Sheepscombe and turning right. The pub is a "free house" offering a wide variety of meals and a range of "real ales". It is a pub in true traditional style and commands a view across the valley, towards Slad, which is unsurpassed.

"Butchers Arms"

Almost immediately there is a bridle way sign where you turn right and start to climb. This is local authors' country and readily identifiable from many of the pages of Laurie Lee's "Cider with Rosie" or steamier passages from the pen of Jilly Cooper.

Pass Rose Cottage on your left and after 100 yards leave the road and take the well used dirt track to your left which climbs quite steeply. Keep the wall and fence on your left and follow the blue arrow signs with a yellow dot.

After a further 100 yards the path divides and you take the path to your left,still following the arrowed route. The path yet again divides and you need to stick to the main track keeping straight ahead. Take your time over this steady climb and enjoy the superb views which are now opening up to your left, of Painswick and the surrounding area.

Eventually the walk begins to flatten out and you are joined by a track coming in from your right. Continue to follow the path at a slight left angle passing a sign for the National Nature Reserve of "Lord's and Lady's Wood" which are protected and cared for by The National Trust. Stay on the main track signed by blue arrow markings.

Follow the path as it climbs gently through the wood, ignoring any other tracks going off right or left. At the top of the climb the path leaves the Nature Reserve and you continue to follow the main track first bearing left then right,with the woods on your left and open fields on your right.

Almost immediately you enter the area of "Saltridge Wood" which is on your left and you have an old dry stone wall on your right. You are now at a high point of the walk with splendid views to your right. In the distance is a radio mast which you will pass later in the walk.

When the dry stone wall goes off to the right, the track divides and you continue to follow the path close to the wall. Very soon the track peters out and you leave the wooded section and go through a wooden gate into a field. Continue straight ahead with a small stone wall on your left.

Cross the field and go through a second wooden gate. As you cross this second field there are paths going off both left and right. Ignore them and continue straight ahead going through a third farm gate.

Enjoy your stroll across this field which offers quite magnificent views to your left. In the foreground is nearby Cranham and in the far distance parts of the Forest of Dean and its famous landmark of May Hill.

Very soon the path joins a farm track where you continue to walk in the same direction. The track then joins a minor country road where you turn right. Take care along here, although it is a village road it is still quite well used. You are now heading for the radio mast that you saw earlier.

After 250 yards leave the road and turn right. Pass Overtown Farm on your right and walk towards the radio mast which you pass on your right. Now follow the blue arrow sign to cross the field at a slight right angle. You are walking in line with the cable posts and heading for a house in the distance.

The bridle way leaves the field through a farm gate and you turn right to walk along the busy B4070 Birdlip to Stroud road for about 300 yards. Again take great care on this road section.

At the bridle way sign, leave the road to the right and walk between the houses to a wooden gate. Again the path divides and you take the blue arrowed track which goes off at a slight left angle.

The bridle way drops steeply down to eventually enter a third section of woodland, called "Workmans Wood" which is also cared for by The National Trust.

Again there are a number of tracks going off both right and left which you have to ignore. Your path through this wonderful wood is well signed with blue arrows painted on the trees. This is a very pleasant walk whatever the season.

"Workmans Wood" is part of the Ebworth estate which was built up by the Ebworth family over the last 100 years. This wood, along with the two earlier woods,was acquired by The National Trust in the 1980's and covers an area of well over 1000 acres. The woods are predominantly beech and ash and are home to a wide variety of flora and fauna.

As you descend through the wood you will find a National Trust Information Post on your right which offers a place to rest and a variety of useful information about both the woods and The Trust.

After the Information Post continue down hill as before, passing two old ponds on your left.

When eventually the wood thins out,the track divides and you take the left fork and follow the track as it sweeps around the field on your left. Very soon the track leaves the wood and passes through a pair of old gates and between some cottages to join a metalled road.

Follow the road, enjoying the sight of fine old cottages alongside it for half a mile, until you arrive back in the centre of Sheepscombe where the "Butchers Arms" stands on your right.

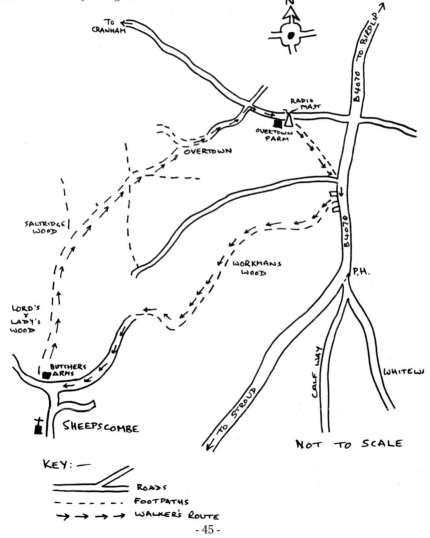

KEY: —

ROADS

-------- FOOTPATHS

→ → → → WALKER'S ROUTE

WALK 16 Stanway to Stanton

Distance: 4 miles Allow: 2[1/2] hours

"A testing walk with a steep start. Thick woodland gives way to open fields with breathtaking views. It is a walk between two beautiful villages and there is a chance to stop off at a memorable pub along the way."

Park you car in the village of Stanway, just off the B4077 Toddington to Stow road and start the walk from the magnificent 17th century gatehouse of Stanway House. The house, which is open to the public on certain days, is a fine Jacobean building complemented by tasteful gardens. The house and the church next to it are well worth a visit.

Leaving the gatehouse behind you and keeping the large estate wall on your left, begin to walk out of the village. After 50 yards leave the road and turn left to follow the "Cotswold Way" signs into the Stanway Estate Yard.

The walk passes close to some fine old houses, the path staying close to the estate wall. Go through a wooden "kissing gate" and take time to note the beautifully carved swan's head looking down on the gate. The path now winds its way to your right, through an old orchard to very soon emerge onto the busy B4077 road.

Turn left and stay on the pavement to follow the road uphill to the top section of the village. Despite the annoying drum of traffic on your right there is a pleasant distraction on this section as you pass by a fine collection of old Cotswold stone cottages.

When the road sweeps off sharply to your right and the pavement peters out, leave the road and continue straight ahead, towards the houses on a narrow country road. Now you need to take great care as the track divides in three directions. After 100 yards ignore the road going left and the road going straight on and take the track between the two, off to the left. This is marked by a blue arrowed bridle way sign but is easily missed.

This is a narrow dirt track and begins to climb quite steeply. At certain times of the year it can get very wet and you need to wear appropriate footwear. Take your time on this section to catch your breath and enjoy the fine views to your left.

You are now entering "Lidcombe Wood" and at the top of the slope is a magnificent beech tree on your right. Here the path divides and you continue straight ahead as the ground flattens out. Behind you and to your left is a fine view over Nottingham Hill.

The path now drops down and meets a farm track where you bear right and after 50 yards, when the path again divides, continue straight ahead. You soon confirm that you are on the right track when you reach a blue arrow marker. This short section again gets very muddy.

You have now reached the steepest part of the walk as the stony path climbs before you. Again find every excuse to stop and catch your breath. "Lidcombe Wood" is home to a wide variety of wild life and is a place to be savoured.

At the top of the bridle way go through a wooden gate and continue to climb for a further 10 yards where you meet a wide track and turn left. The track again climbs steadily uphill and you have a dry stone wall and the woods on your left.

At the top of the slope, when the wood ends the path yet again divides. To your left is a yellow arrowed sign which you ignore and to the right of it a blue arrowed bridle way sign indicating your path across the field.

You are now rewarded for your earlier efforts as the views begin to open up all around you. To your left are several ranges of hills and to your right, green pastures and woodlands. Ahead, you can see Broadway Tower looking protectively down over the town.

Cross two fields and when your path meets a broad track, turn left. Immediately turn left again to follow a wide farm track, keeping a dry stone wall on your left and passing a small stone barn on your right.

At the bottom of the drive the path divides and you have a farmhouse in front of you. Here you turn right following the bridle way to Broadway and make your way around and between the farm barns. Very soon you meet the farm track taking you away from the farm and follow it.

When you leave the farm track the path divides and you turn left following the "Cotswold Way" sign marked Stanton. Here you get the true reward for you efforts. All around you is the most fantastic, panoramic view out across the counties of Worcestershire and Gloucestershire and far beyond. Each range of hills lie before you like a green carpet. In the foreground are the "Malvern Hills" and May Hill, in the distance Hay Bluff and far beyond that the Black Mountain range in South Wales.

Now pass the farmhouse on your left and continue straight ahead to once again pick up the "Cotswold Way" sign and follow its path steeply downhill and to your right, through an avenue of trees. This is a very pretty section but care is needed on the loose stone track. Ahead of you is a magnificent view of Stanton.

At the bottom of the slope follow the yellow arrow sign straight ahead and over a stile then turn sharp right. Walk downhill with the trees on your right, for 150 yards. Here the path goes right, back into the trees and follows a meandering route around and through the trees and passes a small lake on your left.

The path eventually emerges alongside a small waterworks where you join a wide track and turn left. Follow the track which now takes you into the village of Stanton.

The track soon becomes a road and at the 'Y' junction to visit the pub turn sharp right to climb the steep slope to the village pub "The Mount". This is one of the 15 "Donnington" pubs on the "Cotswolds" and offers their famous range of "real ales" and a fine selection of meals. The pub and its garden command a wonderful view over the village and far beyond to Dumbleton Hill, Bredon Hill, the Malverns and the Cleeve Hill escarpement.

To continue walk turn left (from "The Mount" continue downhill) to the village and a chance to step back in time as you pass between a row of lovely old houses, many of which date back to the 17th century. Stanton owes much of its glory to Sir Philip Stott, an architect who bought the estate in 1906 and spent the next 30 years in restoration work.

Walk through the village, passing the stone cross on your right. At the 'T' junction turn left and begin to leave the village. After 200 yards, when the road sweeps round to the right, leave the road and go into a private drive marked Chestnut Farm, following the blue arrow sign towards Stanway.

After a further 100 yards turn right and go over a wooden stile now following the yellow arrowed "Cotswold Way" sign and walk straight ahead. The path crosses a series of fields and stiles and finally emerges after a mile onto a minor country road, where you turn left.

Now follow the road as it takes you back into the village of Stanway and to your car.

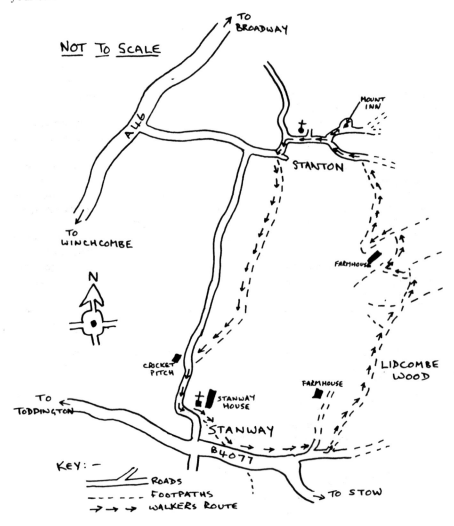

WALK 17 Whittington to Brockhampton

Distance: 4 miles Allow: 2 hours

"An adventurous stroll through open farmland, beginning and ending in one of Gloucestershire's oldest villages. With a varied landscape and a fine old pub for a rest, this is a splendid walk."

Turn off the A40 Cheltenham to Oxford road towards Whittington and park your car to start your walk from the entrance gates to the 16th century Whittington Court.

Cross the minor road with your back to the Court and enter the field through an old "kissing gate". Already the path divides and you take the path to your right, heading towards the A40. The path sweeps around the field and you keep the little stream on your right and then follow the line of the road as you cross the field.

The walking is very flat and easy with good views all around, spoilt only by the constant drum of traffic on the busy main road.

At the far side of the field cross a wooden stile. Continue straight ahead, following the direction of the yellow arrow sign, eventually having a hedge on your left.

When the hedge peters out ignore the blue arrowed bridle way crossing your path and continue to follow the yellow arrowed footpath towards the trees in the distance. Here the path loops around to the right of a pond and is well marked as it passes through a private garden and down a driveway. The garden is well cared for and therefore care is needed not to trespass off the path.

When the driveway meets a minor road, cross over with care and walk up the gravel track directly opposite, keeping a large barn on your left. The path soon divides and the public footpath goes off to the right to avoid a house. Follow the track to pass a garage on your right and a second house on your left and enter a wooded section.

This is a particularly pleasant section and should be savoured. The wood is a quiet place, well stocked with a variety of trees and home to many animals and birds.

When the path leaves the wood, go through a wooden gate and continue straight on over three fields. To your left are fine rural views and below you the infant River Coln, which began life just a few miles away near Cleeve Common.

Very soon you have a dry stone wall on your left and where it ends leave the field through a large metal gate on left and follow the track into Sevenhampton. This is a village of mixed houses, some of which are very old and picturesque.

At the 'T' junction of the road, in the centre of the village, turn left and walk downhill, towards the ford. After 20 yards turn right onto a footpath marked "Brockhampton via St. Andrew's Church", keeping the river on your left.

This pretty section winds its way across the river where you cross a stile and go into a field. Now climb the steep slope ahead and to the right of you, go through the old wooden "kissing-gate". Once again follow the path to your right, towards the church.

When the path meets the minor road cross straight over, now following the sign for Brockhampton through the right hand side of the churchyard. St. Andrew's is a fine old church which is worth visiting now or on your return. Whilst typical of Norman churches all over the area, it was much improved in the 15th century with a gift from a rich wool merchant, John Camber, and has a perpendicular tower named after him.

Leave the churchyard in the far right hand corner through a metal "kissing-gate", keeping the dry stone wall on your left. Cross the field and go through an old wooden gate to cross this second field at a slight right angle, heading for the houses in the far right hand corner.

When you are eventually level with an old brewery chimney look for a metal gate in the dip. Cross the small stream and go through the gate, keeping the dry stone wall on your right. Now follow the path to climb the slope into Brockhampton.

When the path meets a road bear right and you will find the local pub, the "Craven Arms",on your right. You will not be disappointed with your stop as the pub offers a selection of "real ales" and boasts an extensive menu.

From the pub re-trace your steps to St. Andrew's church. Leave the churchyard via the main gate and turn right to climb the steep road out of Sevenhampton.

At the 'T' junction cross straight over the road and go through a large metal gate onto a bridle way and climb the slope. This is a well used track and very soon the views begin to open up to your right over Brockhampton and out towards Winchcombe and Cleeve Common.

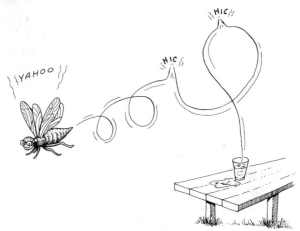

After 300 yards, leave the bridle way and cross a large stile on your left onto a well marked footpath, following the yellow arrow sign. As you steadily climb the hill a fine view opens up to your right over Sevenhampton and its lush, green valley.

Walk diagonally right across field to wooden stile by Iron drinking trough. Cross stile take path right, follow with wall on your left for 50yds at yellow arrow bear left and cross two further fields, eventually emerging on a minor road cross straight over.

right

The path now divides and you follow the marker indicating the path straight ahead, ignoring the path to the left. Follow the well used track, keeping the hedge on your left. Ahead of you and to your left new views begin to open up offering uninterrupted views of Leckhampton Hill and on towards the Forest of Dean.

After 150yds take well marked track to left and begin to make your way down the valley to your left. This section is not marked and you need to take great care.

Stay in the valley basin where you eventually go over a stile which is re-assuredly marked with a yellow arrow. Now loop around to the right of the hedge and make your way along the hedgerow. The path is not well used or marked and you need to look out for some white painted houses below you and to your left.

Eventually the path does re-emerge and drops down along the white houses to take you to the minor road leading into Whittington, where you turn right.

Whittington is again a mixture of old and new houses, some of which are being renovated

At the 'T' junction in the centre of the village turn left and make your way back down the road to the Court and your car.

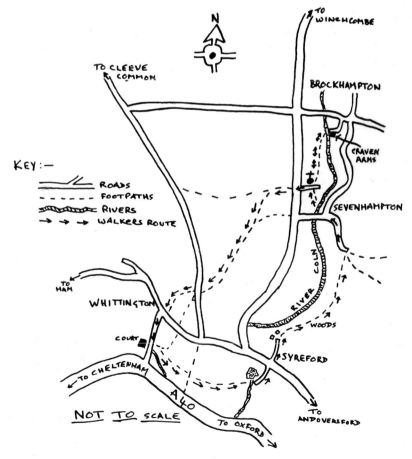

WALK 18 Winchcombe to Postlip

Distance: 4 miles Allow: 2 hours

"A testing ramble along the escarpment of the Cotswolds, starting and ending in one of Gloucestershire's most historic towns. With a steep hill and the reward of wonderful views, this is a walk for the more adventurous rambler."

Before you begin to tackle this walk be warned that several sections of it are prone to being quite muddy so come prepared with an appropriate selection of footwear to suit the season.

Park your car in the centre of Winchcombe and begin the walk from the "Old Corner Cupboard Inn" in Cheltenham Road. This is a Whitbread pub and marks both the start and end of your journey, offering two opportunities to sample its range of food and drink.

The medieval town of Winchcombe has for many years been a popular place for visitors and it is worth adding some time before or after your walk to savour some of its delights.

From the pub, walk out of the town along the B4632 road in the direction of Cheltenham and after a quarter of a mile cross over just before the hospital into a small road directing you to Belas Knap.

BELAS KNAP from the SOUTH

Pass Corndean Lane on your left and walk straight ahead through a "kissing gate" into the field, following a finger post sign pointing you in the direction of Cleeve Common. Already you have the tiny River Isbourne busily flowing alongside you, a river that has the distinction of being one of the few rivers in the country that truly flows northwards.

Very soon the intrusive traffic noises from the busy B4632 begin to die away and are replaced by the more harmonious sounds of the river. At the end of the first field ignore the footpath going off to your left and continue straight ahead after crossing the stile.

When the second field is crossed, go through another "kissing gate" and here the path divides. Ignore the path to your right, join the lane and continue straight ahead. Soon the walk loses its attraction as first you walk through a small residential area and then weave your way through a paper mill. This is Postlip Mill through which the path is well marked with yellow arrows and is easy to follow.

Towards the middle of the complex the path again divides and you should ignore the path to the left and continue through the mill buildings. At the end of site the path yet again divides and this time you follow the arrow signs to the left, taking you up to and through a car park.

The path now goes straight ahead and out of the factory site back into pleasant countryside, offering your first real view of Cleeve Common. Care is now needed as your path takes you slightly left for about 20 yards to cross the narrow waterway over a concrete bridge. Here you turn right and begin to cross several fields, always keeping the hedge on your right.

After crossing three stiles the path takes you along a narrow avenue with spindly trees to your right and a fence on your left. This is the tiny hamlet of Postlip and you are treated to a tantalising view of a row of fine Cotswold stone cottages to your right.

At the end of the path, go up a slight rise to cross another stile to meet a metalled service road. Here you leave the path and turn left onto a path which is also an unmarked bridle way.

As you begin to rise you pass Postlip Hall Farm on your left and head towards The Paddocks. At this point take the opportunity to stop and look back to your right. Below you is the magnificent sight of Postlip Hall itself and beyond it the lush slopes of the Common.

The path continues to climb steadily as you first pass a modern farm and then its outbuildings on your left and all the while are treated to differing views, both left and right. Winchcombe looks like a model town laying in a valley surrounded on all sides by protecting slopes.

Follow the track until it eventually flattens out and begins to drop slightly down hill. Here new views await you as ahead lies a dense wooded section and a cottage in a small clearing. The track now sweeps off to your right and you leave it to go through a metal farm gate on your left.

Your path remains unmarked and you turn sharp right and down the hill, towards the copse, keeping the fence close to your right. Behind you and to your left there are fine view of both Langley and Nottingham Hills and to your right a corner of Cleeve Common and a deep valley.

At the bottom of the slope go through a metal gate cross bridge and take muddy track on right, this is a steady and somewhat steep climb and you should find every excuse to stop and admire the view and catch your breath.

At the top of the slope continue straight ahead, keeping an old dry stone wall on your left. Go over a stile and where the path meets a narrow metalled road, bear left and walk down the road.

The walking is now flat and easy and offers fine views down to your left of Winchcombe with occasional glimpses of Sudeley Castle. Stay on the road for half a mile passing Corndean Hall, a fine old Georgian house, along the way. First mentioned in 1181 the Hall and its land were allegedly transferred to the Abbott of Winchcombe and was used by the monks for recreational purposes.

Just after Corndean Hall you come to a 'Y' junction and continue straight ahead for a further quarter of a mile to a second 'Y' junction, where Belas Knap is marked. Here bear left for about 10 yards and look for a footpath above you and to your left, protected by a large stone stile.

Go over the stile (note strange spelling of Winch(c)ombe on finger post!) and the path immediately divides. Ignore the path to your left marked Postlip and walk straight ahead and down the wide field on a well marked path, heading for Winchcombe at the bottom of the bowl.

As you walk down the field there are magnificent views all around, a true reward for your earlier efforts.

As you near the bottom of the slope, to confirm your route, head directly towards a brown, wooden cricket pavilion before going over a stile to join a metalled service road. Turn right and follow the road out of the private property and into Corndean Lane.

Turn left and, taking great care, follow the lane back towards the B4632 where you turn right to retrace your steps back into Winchcombe and the "Old Corner Cupboard Inn".

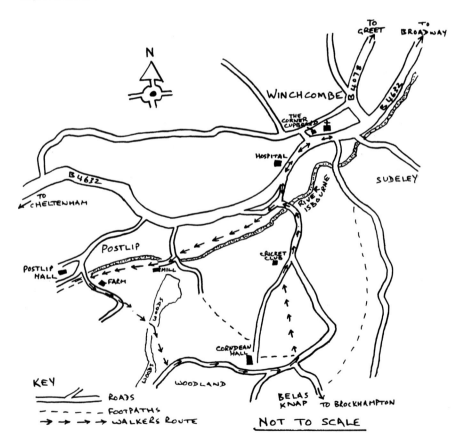

WALK 19 Winchcombe to the Waterhatch

Distance: 5 miles Allow: 3 hours

"A delightfully different walk beginning and ending in one of Gloucestershire's most historic towns,Winchcombe. With a varied landscape and a choice of pubs in the town, this is a walk that you will remember for a long time."

The walk starts in the centre of Winchcombe near the "Plasterers Arms" public house. This is one of many pubs in the ancient town and typical of the cosy welcome awaiting you, either now or on your return.

Winchcombe has a lot to offer the visitor and makes a good centre for touring the "Cotswolds". It was at its most prosperous in medieval times due to its abbey which was founded by King Kenulf of Mercia and dedicated to his martyred son St.Kenelm.

Start your journey by walking away from the car park towards Cheltenham, passing the much photographed row of old Cotswold stone cottages in Dent's Terrace on your left and take the first turning left into Vineyard Street, following the signs for Sudeley Castle. This is a very neat street seen on many postcards and is only spoilt by ever present cars.

Walk down the hill and cross the bridge over the River Isbourne which is one of the few rivers in the country to truly flow northwards.

Continue to the gatehouse of Sudeley Castle and leave the road to the right of the gates to go into the castle grounds, following the signs for the "Wardens' Way", Spoonley and Guiting Wood. As you enter the castle grounds take your time to look back at the fine views of the old "wool" church and the hills beyond.

You are now walking the Chestnut Avenue towards the castle which offers a good day out in its own right. It has a long history with Royal connections dating back to the 10th century. Sudeley is the burial place of Henry VIII's sixth wife, Katherine Parr. Today the castle is renowned for its magnificent gardens and impressive collection of art treasures.

Just before the cattle grid leave the road and turn right to go through a metal farm gate where a sign says "Private Park". You are now following yellow arrows which carry the "Wardens' Way" markings.

Pass the childrens adventure playground and keep close to the fence on your left. Here for the first time you get a view of the ruined section of the castle and a glimpse of its glorious gardens on your left. To the right are splendid views of the foothills leading up to Cleeve Common where the burial mound, Belas Knap, is found.

Go through a "kissing gate" and continue to follow the yellow arrows with the 'W' on, still keeping the fence close on your left. When the fence ends continue straight ahead, towards an old, dead tree.

This well marked path continues at a slight left angle across the field. You are now in a deep bowl with fine views all around and this is a good spot to stop and catch your breath before dropping down to the far left hand corner of the field, where there is a massive tree on your left.

Cross the stream over a little bridge and immediately cross the stile and then bear left. After 20 yards the "Wardens' Way" goes over another stile and straight ahead. Do not cross this stile but turn right to follow a plain yellow arrow mark, keeping a hedge on your left.

The going now is flat and easy. There are lovely views in this lush area which is dotted with fine old houses. At the end of this field cross a wooden stile and continue straight ahead with the fence on your left.

After 150 yards cross a stile on your left, just before a farm gate and turn sharp right to walk down the broad farm track away from the farm buildings. Off to your right are Humblebee Woods and as the track dips down you suddenly come alongside a lake which is a hidden haven for a wide variety of birds.

Go through the metal farm gate and continue to walk up the track as it now rises out of the valley. This is a very pretty section of the walk, thanks in part to the mature trees along the way.

After 300 yards the path divides; follow it for a few yards as it sweeps to the left and then leave it to turn right going into a field. Now cross the field at a slight left angle on a well worn path, towards the trees in the distance.

Go into the copse over a wooden stile and after only a few steps, leave it again over a second stile to continue straight ahead. At the far side of this field cross two further stiles and go straight on. After 20 yards, and just before the trees, bear left and walk up the field, keeping the trees close to your right.

After 300 yards there is a large white disc on your right and it is at this point that you leave the field and enter the woods, using a broad footpath. This is Spoonley Wood and you continue to follow the footpath as it meanders through the wood before suddenly bursting out into a clearing.

In this clearing are the remains of a Roman villa first excavated in the late 19th century. It is a very peaceful place and worth spending a few minutes exploring before moving on through the wood. The layout plan of the 'courtyard' of this villa was used to illustrate the classic text-book *"Everyday life in Roman Britain"*.

The path continues through the clearing and becomes quite narrow as it passes between fir trees. This is a muddy, unmarked section and climbs quite steadily through the trees.

Leave the wood over a wooden stile and very soon the path meets a well established track; here you turn right. The views are once again quite staggering as you follow the track for 300 yards before coming to a 'T' junction where once again you turn right.

The walking is now very easy as you follow the track downhill to the old farm buildings in the valley below. When you arrive at these buildings you pick up a yellow arrow sign with a green and white circle on it signifying that you are on the "Windrush Way". You are now at the Waterhatch and will follow the same way-signs back into Winchcombe.

At the bottom of the slope, where the path divides, bear right and keep the trees on your right. When the track begins to leave the tree line follow it to the left and after 150 yards leave it and turn right at a way-signed post. Now follow the "Windrush Way" signs across the field towards the trees.

The path continues straight ahead, over a series of stiles, always keeping the trees on your right. After 400 yards the path passes between the tree line, over a stile and then goes straight ahead over the middle of the field. Cross another stile and continue across the next field in the same general direction.

At the end of this field Sudeley Castle again comes into view on your right. Leave the field in the far corner, go through a farm gate and after 10 yards turn right onto a stony track and follow the same circular signs.

Cross the stream and a stile, then turn left to immediately cross a second stile. Walk around to your right and cross a brook. Now walk straight ahead across a field following the well marked path towards the castle, until you rejoin the private drive that takes you back into Winchcombe to complete your journey.

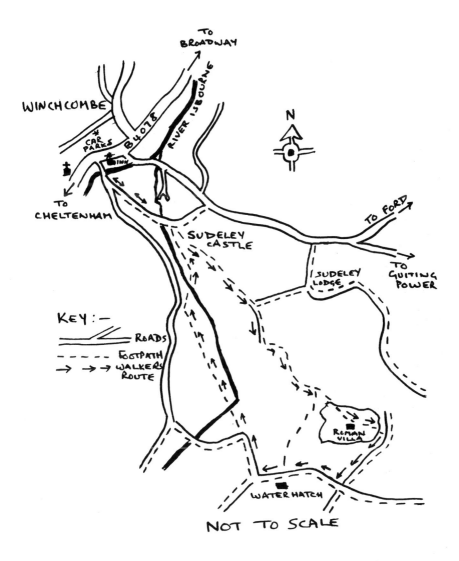

NOT TO SCALE

WALK 20 Yanworth to Fossebridge

Distance: 3[1/2] miles Allow: 2 hours

"A walk through open farmland, with the pretty River Coln for company. With a varied landscape and a pub for a rest halfway, this is a delightful walk."

Park the car in Yanworth village and start the walk from St. Michael's Church, which stands on the eastern edge of the village. The church is well worth a visit; standing between splendid farm buildings, it boasts an impressive wall painting of "Old Father Time" complete with scythe.

The views from the church and farm are already magnificent as you gaze over a deep lush valley, green and inviting and tailor made for the walker.

From the church walk to your left and then to the right of the imposing Tythe Barn and pass between this and the stables, on a metalled farm road which sweeps right behind the buildings. Now follow the road away from the farm downhill until you meet a minor country road where you turn left and continue downhill.

The views remain quite stunning as you make your way carefully along the road, ignoring the footpath going off to your left. Stay on the road as it sweeps around to the left and stay on it as it steadily rises to a 'T' junction. Here you turn right towards Fossebridge and Chedworth and walk down the road until it sweeps right by a small cottage.

At the far side of the cottage leave the road and take the footpath into the field on your left which takes you off at a right angle across the field and into the valley. As you cross the field you are passing through the grounds of Stowell Park, the home of Lord and Lady Vestey. A glance over your left shoulder will reveal the house itself, perched on the hilltop above you.

The footpath now leads you into the valley basin to briefly walk alongside the fast flowing waters of the pretty River Coln, which sprang to life in the nearby Cleeve hills and is halfway in its frantic race to join the mighty Thames.

Shortly after crossing a small brook the way parts company with the river and you need to begin to head to the left of the large clump of trees ahead of you.

Just before the end of the field go through a farm gate on your left and immediately turn right to keep the dry stone wall on your right. Now walk straight ahead towards the conifers which you eventually pass on your right.

You now have a steady climb ahead of you and should find every excuse to stop and catch your breath and enjoy the fine views that continue to open up to your left.

At the end of the wood go through the farm gate, bear left across the field making for a further gate, which leads into the woods opposite. Before entering the woods you are treated to a truly lovely view down to your right along the valley leading towards Chedworth.

Go though the gate and after 10yds, turn right onto an old concrete path, and follow this path until it exits the woods through an iron gate. Turn right and follow the path round one bend, then continue forwards ignoring any paths going left or right. Re-enter the woods, the path snakes its way through sparse woodlands and leaves through a wooden gate. The views have now changed again and you are looking down into a deep valley in which nestles your port of call, the "Fossebridge Inn".

Walk down the slope of the field in the general direction of the main road, enjoying a fine view to your right, back over the River Coln, as you do so. The bridle way leaves the estate in the bottom left hand corner where you go through a large pair of wooden gates. Now turn right and very carefully make your way alongside the busy A429 road and over the river bridge where you will find the pub.

The "Fossebridge Inn" offers a pleasant resting place before you continue on your journey. The pub boasts a wide menu and a good choice of beers and has the added attraction of a beer garden right alongside the Coln.

From the pub turn right and at the end of the building leave the 'A' road and take the well marked footpath that runs along a narrow passage between the pub and a house. After 200 yards the path emerges onto a minor country road where you turn right and stay on the road for about half a mile, as you pass through a small hamlet. Once again you are in open country you are treated to a fine valley view along the River Coln, home to a variety of wildlife, including moorhens, ducks, coots and swans.

A Mallard Duck

A Moorhen

The Great Crested Grebe

Fifty yards after a 'T' junction leave the road and turn right, following a footpath sign across the field to walk alongside the river. At the far side of the field, do not cross the river bridge but look for a small stone stile in the wall ahead of you which you now cross and walk straight ahead.

The path is sandwiched between the hedge and the river and you keep close to the hedge and eventually pass alongside a copse on your left. Now is the time to enjoy a final view of Stowell Park, on the hillside on your right. It is easy to see how imaginative our forefathers were in their sighting of these fine houses.

At the end of this field continue straight ahead in the same direction heading towards a large farmhouse. Leave the field through a large gate just to the left of the farm and walk up to the road where you turn right.

Walk up the minor road to pass a fine old mill building on your left and just beyond this leave the road by taking the footpath on your left. This path takes you diagonally across the field to join another minor road which you join and follow uphill retracing your earlier steps to Yanworth to complete your journey.

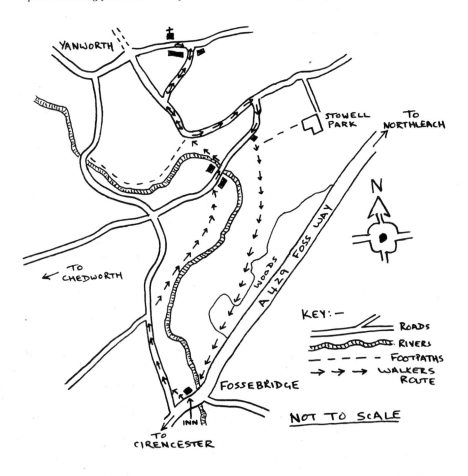